# JERSEY BUSES

## IAN JORDAN

AMBERLEY

*Front cover (top):* 4 (J47 452), operated by Tantivy Blue Coach Tours, is seen on a Saturday afternoon in August awaiting the arrival of tourists to transport them to their hotels for their holiday on the island.

*Front cover (bottom): Oliver* (J14 672, formerly 128 DTD) was acquired by Pioneer Coaches in late 1992 and was converted to open-top in February 1993 for a service launched on the island in the summer of that year.

*Back cover*: Connex took over the operation of the island's bus services in September 2002. 247 (J10 1747) was one of a number of second-hand buses to be acquired when the company noticed that the thirty-three brand new Darts would not be enough to cope with the summer tourist season. 247 was placed in service in its former operator's livery while the others were being made ready for service along with some hired buses.

First published 2022

Amberley Publishing
The Hill, Stroud
Gloucestershire, GL5 4EP

www.amberley-books.com

Copyright © Ian Jordan, 2022

The right of Ian Jordan to be identified as
the Author of this work has been asserted in
accordance with the Copyrights, Designs and
Patents Act 1988.

ISBN 978 1 3981 1077 9 (print)
ISBN 978 1 3981 1078 6 (ebook)

British Library Cataloguing in Publication Data.
A catalogue record for this book is available from
the British Library.

Origination by Amberley Publishing.
Printed in the UK.

# Introduction

The Channel Islands are a small group of islands situated in the English Channel off the Normandy coast of France. Jersey is the largest of the islands and is a popular tourist destination, being only an hour's flight from the United Kingdom. It was also made famous by the BBC drama programme *Bergerac*.

Jersey has a favourable climate with numerous bays and beaches, and attractions such as Jersey Zoo, which opened in 1959, becoming home to Durrell Wildlife Conservation Trust in the mid-1960s. Jersey is home to the annual Battle of Flowers Parade, which takes place on the second Thursday in August. The parade would not only include the odd bus or two, but some of the floats were built on former bus or coach chassis.

Jersey provides a comprehensive network of bus and coach services for residents and holidaymakers alike, with enhanced services serving the popular bays and beaches operating during the summer months. The main bus operator in this era was Jersey Motor Transport (JMT), accompanied by six main coach operators – Blue Coach Tours, Holiday Tours, Mascot Coaches, Pioneer Coaches, Tantivy Motor Tours and Waverley – with each operating twenty to forty coaches and minibuses. There is also a handful of smaller operators. A big change occurred in 1993 when Holiday Tours, Mascot Coaches and Tantivy Motor Tours merged to form Tantivy Holiday Tours, operating a fleet of over 100 coaches and minibuses. Although the fleets reduced in size over the following years due to a fall in tourist numbers as a result of hotel and attraction closures, a small notable change happened in 1995 when new operator Classic Coaches started using three vintage coaches on island tour work. In 1997, Blue Coach Tours and Tantivy Holiday Tours merged to form Tantivy Blue Coach Tours.

The buses then in operation dated from the 1970s and were mainly Fords, bodied by either Willowbrook or Duple. These were joined in the 1980s by a number of Vanguard-bodied buses, which were the first automatic buses for the island. Coaches were Bedfords with Duple bodywork. Bus and coach widths needed to be limited due to narrow roads and weight restrictions, but as suitable sized vehicles were unavailable, the islands restrictions had to be modified to allow the use of modern buses and coaches. This also meant finding someone who could build a suitable vehicle, as those used on the mainland as welfare vehicles lacked the luggage space necessary to transport holidaymakers from the airport and ferry terminals to and from their hotels.

All bus routes in Jersey radiated from the capital, St Helier, which meant that, unless touring the island by coach, passengers would need to return via St Helier to change buses in order to reach another destination on a different route. However, in the late 1990s, this changed following the introduction of route 8B, which linked the Living Legend with Jersey Pearl, the zoo and Gorey for the pier and potteries. Consisting of a single lunchtime round trip, this cut across the middle of the island so that intending passengers would not need to go via St Helier, nor transfer buses there. Most of the services operated are hourly, with the exception of those to Gorey, the airport and local town services. However, the demand during the summer months would prompt duplicates, and on occasions a third vehicle, to cope with loadings, especially on the morning services around 10 a.m. out of St Helier for those wanting to enjoy a day out.

Two other operators provided passenger transport on the island. One used three Second World War DUKWs linking West Pier and Elizabeth Castle – when the tide was in everyone needed to use the DUKWs to get to and from the castle. The other was three road trains, which provided a service around the town via the Fort Regent leisure centre. The second service ran along the beach wall path between West Pier and St Aubin's Bay.

By 2003 (the end of this book's scope), tourist numbers were on the increase again with the recent building of a couple of seafront hotels, apartments and the Waterfront complex. JMT lost its bus service licence to Connex in September 2002. Tantivy Blue Coach Tours, the parent company of the former JMT, were awarded a licence for a hop-on/hop-off coach service. They used the Easylink name for the summer 2003 season and a fleet of Dennis Darts – made surplus with the loss of the bus services. I noted during August 2003 that if Easylink had not been awarded a licence then the service operated by Connex would not have been sufficient to cope as they did not have enough capacity or duplicate buses to meet the high season demand.

I found all operators enthusiast friendly and helpful, and most operators provided me with current, up-to-date fleet information, except Connex, but the information provided by office staff at the time gave me the detailed information I needed.

If you have never visited Jersey and was thinking a visit is overdue then I would recommend it. As most places are closed on a Sunday then this day can be used for one of the 'Round the Island' coach tours, which would then enable you to use the local buses for the rest of your stay to go back to some of the places either passed or visited on the tour, thus letting you see the island at its best.

# Jersey Motor Transport (t/a JMT Express and Jersey Bus)

Jersey Motor Transport (JMT), Jersey's own bus company, used both the trading names of JMT Express and Jersey Bus during the period this book covers.

The buses used a blue and white fleet livery and were known for their all-over adverts not only advertising local attractions and businesses but also cigarettes and beer or lager brands (a variety are shown within the pages of this book). The company operated Fords with Willowbrook, Duple and later Vanguard bodywork. These were joined by four MCW Metroriders in 1988 and in 1991 by five Leyland Vanguards. In 1994, following a slight length restriction relaxation, a batch of five Dennis Darts joined the fleet with repeat orders following in 1995/7/8 replacing older buses in the fleet.

Twenty-five services were operated at the start of the 1988 summer season; this had reduced to nineteen services in the 2002 summer season. A renumbering of services took place in October 1988.

A total of sixty-three buses made up the fleet, using fleet numbers 1–64 (the number 13 was never used). By 1998 the number of buses had reached sixty-eight, using numbers up to 69.

A joint venture with Jersey Electricity from 1 June 1999 saw the purchase of four former City of Oxford electric Optare Metroriders. Three of these were used on a new town circular service, numbered 88 and running every 10 minutes between 9.30 a.m. and 4.50 p.m. with a flat fare of 20p. These were numbered E1–E3, but were more often off the road than on due to their reliability. The service on route 88 was operated using the company's own Metroriders. The service was soon discontinued and the buses withdrawn.

A further six second-hand Dennis Darts joined the fleet from the Isle of Man in 2000. The company lost the contract to operate the island's bus services from September 2002 following the award to Connex bus services.

Most of the remaining buses in the fleet passed to parent company Tantivy Blue Coach Tours and most, except the twenty-six Dennis Darts, were disposed for scrap, with a handful (Nos 17, 18, 20, 23, 25 and 42) being shipped to Guernsey for use at the island games. The twenty-six Dennis Darts were then used for a new service.

JMT1 (J20499), one of a number of Fords with Willowbrook bodywork, is parked up on the pavement at the Weighbridge terminus. This bus dates from 1975 and is one of the oldest buses in the fleet. It was thirteen years old when this photo was taken in June 1988. These buses would park up after school work, or were spare from the depot, so the controllers could see from the offices what spare buses were around if any were needed for duplication.

JMT3 (J20503) is seen at the Weighbridge terminus in St Helier after returning from a morning school journey. The bus carries advertising livery for drinks company Corona and has been in this livery for at least six years. This photo was taken in June 1988 and the bus would only provide service for a couple more months as, in August of the same year, it was destroyed by fire.

JMT5 (J20473) is seen in its Occupation Museum livery – one of the popular tourist attractions., along with the German underground hospital. The driver, having just done a school run, has set the destination blind ready for its next trip but has yet to set the route number blind for his next journey.

JMT15 (J58924), one of the Duple-bodied Ford's dating from 1978, is seen in an all-over advert for one of Jersey's original breweries – Randall's, which dates back to 1819 and has many pubs located around the island. The bus is seen at the Weighbridge bus station, which would see a new layout later that year.

JMT21 (J42653) is seen in the north-west of the island at Grave de Lecq on route 8 (by 1990 this was renumbered route 9), just over 30 minutes from St Helier. This location has a popular café that leads onto the beach, plus there is plenty of evening entertainment. The bus advertises Silk Cut, another cigarette brand available at many of the duty-free warehouses on the island.

JMT24 (J34191) is about to depart from the bus station on route 15 to the airport, via St Aubin and Red Houses. It is seen in this yellow and brown Benson & Hedges advert livery. Tobacco products were one of the most advertised goods on the island's buses, along with wine and spirits.

JMT35 (J29710) is seen after having not long arrived on route 15. The bus carries this beige livery for Le Riches, a seller of foods and wine established in 1818. The company lasted until 2002, when the company merged with another retailer.

JMT36 (J29713) Gala Holidays is one of the tourist companies that operates package tours to the Channel Islands (using holiday tours for excursions and airport transfers). This orange livery is the second version that was carried by this bus; the previous version was a pink-based livery with the same wording. The bus was returned to fleet livery in April 1996.

JMT3 (J70700) is seen in a white-based livery for Top Personnel, an agency founded in 1975 and based in St Helier. The bus was one of four Metroriders taken into stock in 1988.

JMT9 (J33627) is seen about to undertake a duplication on route 8A to the German Underground Hospital, Strawberry Farm and Fantastic Gardens. Some of the duplicates would be provided as extras at the time of normal timetabled journeys or, if the number of passengers at the bus stop was more than a bus load prior to departure, the bus would be slotted in. These would not always run the full route and sometimes resulted in passengers having to transfer buses if there was enough space at the first place of interest, allowing the duplication to return to the bus station should it be needed elsewhere.

JMT12 (J31120) the Flying Flower company was run from the indoor market in the town of St Helier. In 1990, this bus carrying their advert in a rather eye-catching green and white striped livery. Not only were the company's flowers of good quality, they were reasonably priced too.

JMT18 (J40853) was seen in a white-based livery for JPS (John Player Special) cigarettes in the late 1980s and early 1990s. Because of the island being duty free, many wine/spirit and tobacco companies advertised on the buses of the fleet. Another for Raffles 100s can be seen behind.

JMT16 (J33704) is about to depart on an extra trip to another popular Jersey tourist destination – the zoo. It carries a dark and light brown livery for Benson & Hedges special filter cigarettes.

To mark forty-five years of liberation, JMT29 (J43048) received an all-over advert for the German Underground Hospital in 1990. The bus is about to depart for a trip to Gorey Pier.

This shows the rear end of the advert on JMT29 (J43048). The old JMT depot and offices can be seen in the background.

JMT31 (J14644) is seen parked between duties on town route 19. It carries the red and white version of the Raffles Kings and 100s advert; other buses with this advert are black and white.

JMT45 (J70712) is seen at the Wweighbridge bus station having just returned from the Devil's Hole on route 7, a place served by bus every 2 hours, with an hourly afternoon journey so visitors would be able to get back to their hotels in time for the evening meals.

JMT54 (J58128) is ready for its departure to Gorey Pier via St Clement's inner road. It carries a white and yellow livery for Schweppes lemonade.

JMT64 (J31312) is seen in an advert for Rossborough insurance company, which dates from 1944 and offers, among other things, car insurance, which this bus is advertising. It makes use of the wheels with them representing the car wheels on one of two different versions of the livery. It is about to depart St Helier on route 1A.

In 1991, five new Leyland Swifts arrived with Vanguard bodywork to replace old Willowbrook-bodied Fords. JMT1 (J15374) is seen on route 1 about to take another full load of passengers to Gorey Pier from St Helier.

JMT5 (J15908) is another of the 1991 deliveries. It is seen ready to depart to L'Etacq on route 12A, which also serves Jersey Gold, another popular tourist attraction.

JMT9 (J33627) is looking fresh from a recent repaint. It is seen at the Weighbridge bus station with passengers waiting to board the 10.50 departure on route 7 to the Devil's Hole.

Launching on 15 March 1982, BBC Radio Jersey celebrated its tenth anniversary in 1992 and had this advertising livery applied to mark the occasion. JMT11 (J32066) is seen in August 1993 parked up in the bus parking area across the road from Weighbridge bus station.

By 1993 most of the Ford-bodied Willowbrooks were mainly confined to school work, with the odd one seen on duplications; for example, JMT14 (J33617), seen here parked up and waiting to see if it's needed.

JMT18 (J40853) is about to depart with a full load to the popular St Brelade's Bay on route 14. JMT18 is a Ford with Vanguard bodywork and operating its seventh year on the island.

JMT21 (J42653) is seen operating an extra service on the 8A, though possibly only as far as the German Underground Hospital. This was taken around 10.30 a.m. in August 1993.

The Living Legend, the former Fantastic Gardens tourist attraction, is served by route 8A. JMT22 (J33703) had just worked this route when it was seen here at the Weighbridge bus station in this white-based advert livery telling us there is 'fun for all the family'.

JMT26 (J43066) is seen about to depart on the 11 a.m. departure of route 4 to Bonne Nuit Bay, a small, quiet little bay 31 minutes out of St Helier.

Jersey Gold is a tourist attraction 40 minutes from St Helier on route 12A. JMT30 (J14639) advertises it in this all-over yellow and black advert livery promoting the chance to win a car. The bus is awaiting its driver for a trip out to Jersey Zoo, a journey that takes 19 minutes.

Jersey Pearl is another attraction on the island, on route 5. JMT31 (J14644) advertises it with this maroon-based livery, seen after having arrived back from a route 15 journey from the airport.

JMT33 (J14650) is seen at the Weighbridge bus station ready for its departure to St Brelade's Bay. It carries a white-based advert for Rossborough's insurance company, this time using a silver car on the side advertising pensions rather than car insurance.

JMT37 (J29717) is seen at Weighbridge bus station having just arrived from Gorey. The driver has already set his destination ready for his trip on route 12A to L'etacq. This bus has either just lost its advert or is about to gain the rest of its advert when the bus is available.

JMT40 (J15079) is providing an extra journey on route 8A due to the number of passengers wanting to visit either the Living Legend or the Underground Hospital.

JMT41 (J42252) is seen between trips in the parking area at the Weighbridge bus station. It is carrying an advert livery for Raffles 100s, telling us it's a terrific deal.

JMT42 (J42259) is seen arriving at Gorey Pier on route 1A. The bus has the large JMT Express fleet names with black window surrounds.

JMT44 (J15031) is seen at the Weighbridge bus station about to depart to L'Etacq. It has an all-over advert for the Samare's Manor at St Clements, which is a botanic garden and self-catering cottages with an award-winning restaurant, offering fun for the whole family.

JMT45 (J70712) is about to depart on a journey to the Devil's Hole on route 7. This Metrorider is white and awaiting an advert in this 1991 view.

JMT48 (J16439) is about to work an extra to the zoo on route 3. This is a destination that normally requires an extra bus on the first of the morning trips. Buses are monitored in the afternoon to see how many people arrive back on the earlier buses so they know if an extra bus is needed to get people back to their hotels and guesthouses in time for their evening meal.

JMT50 (J71210) is seen in full JMT Express livery while parked up at the Weighbridge bus station.

JMT52 (J58923) is blinded for its next trip on route 8. Around half the fleet is allocated the workings for the season at the start of the timetable. A full list of these were displayed in the information office, which made it easy to know when certain vehicles would be around, allowing for a number of buses to be spare every day to cater for services that needed extra capacity and others to cover for buses that are off the road for various reasons.

JMT56 (J58127) has just arrived from St Brelade's Bay and is setting down its passengers as the driver waits to depart. The bus has a dual advert in a white-based livery for B. G. Romeril & Co., which offers products and services for the home, along with Twyford Bathrooms, which has been trading on the island for over forty years.

JMT57 (J16527) seen in Gorey on route 1b. Gorey is a popular destination with a small harbour. Gorey castle is one of the village's attractions, as well as walks across the top of the island, where most of the Jersey Royal potatoes are grown.

JMT59 (J16598) is seen loading up for its journey to Gorey Pier and is in full JMT livery, but has writing for the newly opened Marks & Spencer's store at the airport. This will be their third store on the island, with one at St Helier and the other at Red Houses.

JMT63 (J31300) is providing an extra journey for the few passengers that the previous image's JMT59 left behind on this morning run out to Gorey Pier. Gorey held a fête each year around the time of the Battle of Flowers, which would have a few stalls with items for sale and the usual raffles.

JMT64 (J31312) is seen leaving St Helier on its way to the airport. This route, along with the Gorey routes, was the most frequent on the island. Bus 64 was the highest in the fleet at the time the photo was taken, which would change over the next few years, as will be seen later in this book.

The arrival of the first Dennis Darts on the island gave way for new weight restrictions, allowing the company to buy replacements to replace buses coming up to twenty years old. JMT8 (J46631) is seen advertising the hire shops where, according to the slogan on the bus, you can hire virtually anything.

JMT51 (J46828) is seen having just arrived into the bus station. It is seen dropping off its passengers and has its dot matrix blind set ready for its journey to Bouley Bay. The bus replaced a Ford Willowbrook and is seen with the Jersey Bus fleet name.

JMT4 (J46598), delivered new in June 1994, is seen ready for its journey to the airport on route 15 in August 1995. It had this red and white Coca-Cola advert applied in April of the same year. This bus was also featured on a phone card at the time, but unlike my photo the left-hand corner was red.

JMT7 (J75609) is seen in this green-based advert livery for Bavaria lager and is parked up ready for its next departure to L'Etacq on route 12A.

JMT44 (J84709) is parked up and ready for its departure to St John's Church. The bus was advertising for Tailor, the island's only recruitment company for 'temps'. The second photo shows the nearside of the same bus while parked up in the bus station.

JMT6 (J46744) was delivered in June 1994. It had this all-over advert for Ribena applied in December 1995 and is seen at St Brelade's Bay on route 14 in August 1997.

JMT6 (J46744) is about to depart to St John's Church. We can see an offside view of the Ribena advert.

JMT11 (J13853) is seen operating the town service 18, which uses two buses and runs every 20 minutes. It not only serves the Le Marais estate, but also serves the shops from the far end of the town, including duty-free wine warehouses.

JMT22 (J74393) is loading passengers for Corbiere and the lighthouse in the evening. The driver of the last bus was aware that visitors to the island would go out to get photos of the sun setting over the lighthouse and would pick up passengers down the hill rather than them having to walk back up to the bus stop. The last bus left St Helier at 8.20 p.m. and Corbiere at 9 p.m.

Here we see JMT22 (J74393) at Greve de Lecq awaiting its departure time before heading back to the capital.

Joining JMT11 on the town service for the summer schedules is JMT47 (J6926747), seen here awaiting its relief driver.

Seen here is JMT65 (J86370). For a number of years JMT wanted more than the sixty-three buses it had to cope with loading in the busy summer months. This was now possible with the reduction of coaches and the amount of PSV and charabanc vehicles allowed on the island. Most of the older buses in the fleet have now been replaced.

JMT65 (J86370) is seen approaching the Gorey Pier terminus of route 1B having worked its way through from St Helier.

JMT66 (J86372) was the highest in the fleet when this photo was taken. It is about to leave St Helier for the zoo.

By 1999, after about ten years, JMT3 (J70700) had lost its white base with orange and black sign writing livery for this rather bright orange version for Top Personnel. It is also seen covering for an electric Metrorider on the short-lived 88 town circular service.

JMT4 (J46598) had lost its red and white Coca-Cola advert for a slightly different version of the new bright Top Personnel livery due to it been a longer bus. It is seen awaiting its driver for departure on route 12 to Corbiere in August 1999.

JMT14 (J33617) and JMT66 (J86372), old and new, are seen in St Helier bus station in between trips. JMT14 is now providing school transport rather than its old routine of frontline work some twenty-four years ago.

JMT20 (J43037) is seen in the second of the three versions of Top Personnel livery. It carries more orange than first applied to JMT3 in the late 1980s but with white, unlike the 1999 version.

By 1999, JMT39 (J40899) had gained this yellow-based advert for drinks company Schweppes, or should that be 'Schhh you know who?' The bus is seen at Living Legend about to take passengers back to St Helier after they have visited the attraction.

JMT40 (J61334) is seen with its Jersey Bus fleet name while awaiting time for a journey to Plemont on route 8.

JMT67 (J64745) is getting ready to take passengers to the Living Legend on route 8A on this overcast day.

JMT69 (J11467) would be the highest and newest bus in the JMT fleet, giving the company a total of sixty-eight buses. This allowed for a few services to have slight adjustments to the timetables. The bus is seen loading for its journey to the airport via St Aubin's and Red Houses.

E2 (J34139, ex-L802HJO), ex-City of Oxford, was acquired in partnership with Jersey Electric to provide a service every 10 minutes linking the town in a shape of eight and running as Hoppa 88. The service and its buses were soon withdrawn due to their unreliability.

E3 (J13786, ex-H804HJO) is another of the four ex-Oxford buses acquired for the experimental electric trail on Hoppa 88. Only three of the four entered service, but it was withdrawn without replacement and the electric buses were sold. E3 is seen parked up ready to start its service on the route for the day.

JMT28 (J70708) is seen in St Helier in a white and green livery for PBS, a supplier of office products and business solutions since 1972. The bus has a stack of Hoppa leaflets in the window, suggesting that it had been in use (or going to be used) on the service. This was the first Metrorider to be scrapped in August 2000.

JMT50 (J71210) is seen passing the Weighbridge bus station while covering for an electric bus on the short-lived town Hoppa route 88.

This colourful advert on JMT8 (J46631), seen at St Brelade's Bay on route 14, is for the local branches of the Co-Op food store using a smart red, green and yellow livery. Unfortunately the bus saw little use in the two weeks that I was on the island and this was the only chance I had to get a photograph of the bus in this advert.

JMT2 (J58917) is a Ford Duple-bodied bus. It has its blinds set for its next departure on route 1A on another sunny August morning. The bus is seen in standard fleet livery with the later Jersey Bus fleet name.

JMT5 (J15908) is one of five Leyland Swifts delivered in 1991. It has just arrived back at the Weighbridge bus station after its journey from the airport. It has a white sign written-based livery for Jersey Telecom, telling us that a 30-minute phone call is still 7p – the same as five years ago. The front of the bus still carries the later company fleet name.

Having lost its Ribena advert, Dennis Dart JMT6 (J64744) received this Contravision advert for one of Jersey's popular tourist attractions, the Living Legend, which was promoting the fact that actor John Nettles, famous for playing the Channel Island detective in the BBC's *Bergerac*, tells the story of the island to visitors.

JMT10 (J46794) is seen at St Aubin outside the former police station in a blue-based livery for Steeple Finance Limited while working a route 15 to the airport.

JMT11 (J13853) is seen in this white and red livery for Aficio. The company sold digital copiers, printers and fax machines by Ricoh. The bus has full load of passengers ready to enjoy a trip to Greve de Lecq on route 9.

Having returned to the bus station, the driver of JMT12 (J75153) has set the blinds for its next trip on route 1 to Gorey Pier. It carries this all-over advert for Funland amusement arcade on the esplanade, which was the only family arcade on the island that was in the town – the only other amusements were at Fort Regent. The side entrance to the arcade was near the old Waverley Coaches depot. By 2003 the arcade had closed and the Waverley depot had moved to the former Pioneer premises to allow for redevelopment and office blocks to be built.

JMT16 (J75197) is seen at the bus station about to work a route 12 to Corbiere Lighthouse after a shower of rain. It is another in Steeple Finance livery and identical to JMT10.

JMT16 (J75197) is about to operate the 3A to Jersey Zoo, having returned from its trip on route 12.

JMT19 (J15884) seen in the bus station about to work route 1A on a morning journey. Note the driver's cash bag in the window, which was used rather than the usual cash tray.

JMT22 (J74393) is seen in this smart, eye-catching advert for the *Jersey Evening Post*, the island's own newspaper, which is now available online. This bus was the second one in Contravision advert livery. Passengers are waiting for the departure to the Living Legend, which the other bus with the Contravision ad also advertises.

JMT23 (J43063) has been allocated to town service route 19 for its 1999 summer schedules. It is seen at the bus station awaiting its next departure.

JMT24 (J34191) is seen in 1999 at the entrance of the JMT bus garage at the former abattoir, ready to take up its day's allocation.

JMT25 (J43085) is seen about to depart on route 1B to Gorey Pier with another full load. By this time most buses were in fleet livery rather than advert livery following the ban of tobacco product advertising.

JMT27 (J75241) is about to take up a journey to the Living Legend on route 8A in an all-over advert for Roy Scot, a finance company that started trading in 1994.

JMT29 (J43048), another of the Ford Vanguards in the fleet, is about to take up service on route 12A to L'Etacq.

JMT33 (J14650) is providing an extra on route 8A. When extras are provided the buses do not always operate the full route. With route 8A it was possible that if the service bus had room to accommodate the passengers after the Underground Hospital, the bus would then return to St Helier to be ready if needed to provide additional extra journeys elsewhere. In addition to this, it was possible that afternoon extras would run empty from the bus station to the Underground Hospital if the driver had notified the controller that he was leaving the Living Legend with a full load. As with the morning journey extras provided to get people to their destinations for the day, the company would also make sure there was enough space for those getting back to hotels for evening meals or even excursions.

JMT34 (J29709) had arrived back from its journey to Corbiere Lighthouse and awaits its next journey once its driver has taken his break. The bus carries the new Jersey Bus fleet names while the bus next to it still has the JMT Express ones.

JMT38 (J58921), having worked a morning school route, is seen parked up and waiting to provide additional transport if it is needed on this rather wet day.

JMT43 (J42298) is seen providing an extra to Jersey Zoo. Another point worth noting was that when extras were provided some departed before the scheduled departure, but they would also be direct so would not always go out via the route that was about to leave, so a route 3 could be the next departure but the extra would go via the quickest route.

JMT46 (J16043) is already eight years old and is about to depart for L'Etacq on route 12A. The bus carries the latest fleet names.

JMT49 (J64744) is seen with this rather bright advert on behalf of the Jersey road safety panel telling people not to drive after taking drugs or drinking, but to use public transport instead. The driver has set the blinds ready for his next journey on route 3 to Rozel Bay.

JMT51 (J46828) carries a white-based livery on this Dennis Dart, which was used for advertising Channel Island Chicken. Like most places in the 1990s there was a chicken shop named after various places or different styles, and the Channel Islands are no exception, as seen here on JMT51 about to work the 5 to St Mary's Church.

JMT57 (J16527) is seen parked up between runs at the Weighbridge bus station.

JMT61 (J31271) is seen in April 1995. Park Personnel, founded in 1979, used a bright yellow-based livery to advertise its services, which can be seen here on JMT61 at Weighbridge bus station while waiting to be used on a route 19 journey.

JMT62 (J31281) carried this blue-based livery for Emeraude Lines Ferries, a company formed in 1977, a year before this bus arrived on the island, advertising its day trips to St Malo.

JMT66 (J86372) carries one of the last adverts to be applied to a JMT bus, and the very last advert bus I ever took a picture of. JMT66 is in livery for the AA Team recruitment consultants and is seen on town service route 18. It is at Weighbridge, having only been completed the night before. This image was taken 20 minutes before my coach left to take us to the airport, ending our 1999 holiday and the last time I would visit the island with Jersey Motor Transport operating.

Coca-Cola has a long connection with advertising on Jersey buses, with a different advert each time I visited the island. 1999 was no exception, as seen here on JMT68 (J85325) at St Aubin while working a route 14 to St Brelade's Bay, this time using a coke bottle on its side.

# Blue Coach Tours

This coach operator used Bedford Coaches with Duple bodywork in a two-tone blue livery. Some Leyland Elme coaches were added at a later date. A single Iveco coach was notable within the fleet, while minibuses were mainly Volkswagen Transporters and Ford Transits. There are full day tours of the island plus half-day visits to places of interest, which operated on Sunday to Friday as on a Saturday. Coaches and drivers are needed to transfer tourists to and from the airport or ferry terminals and hotels.

Blue Coach Tours 45 (J10603) is seen just outside the town of St Helier, at the coach park near the old abattoir, and is one of many Bedfords in the fleet. The coaches would use this parking area before departing on whole-day or half-day excursions.

# Classic Coaches

A new company operating three classic coaches and offering vintage tours. Classic Coaches started in 1995 and operated for at least three seasons, providing around the island tours or a private hire of a vintage coach. They also operated a service on behalf of the Jersey museums, linking their sites for visitors. The coaches were all Bedfords, with the oldest dating from 1937 and used on the museums service in the then livery of Tantivy Motors. The other two were Bedford OBs, which used a cream livery with a red relief.

Classic Coaches Bedford OB (J5149) is seen arriving for its lunchtime stop at Grave de Lecq on its full day tour of the island with a full load. This was one of two Bedford OBs operated by the company.

Classic Coaches 1937 Bedford (J8588) was used exclusively on tours for visitors to the museum to take guests to the other buildings. It is seen parked up outside the museum in the morning ready for its day's work.

# Holiday Tours, Mascot Motors and Tantivy Motors Tours

Holiday Tours, Mascot Motors and Tantivy Motors Tours merged to form one company in 1993, which had over a hundred coaches. Each company used mainly Bedfords, with the others being Leylands, plus Volkswagen Transporters and Toyota mini-coaches. Each provided their own tours around the island, along with hotel transfers. A coach from each of the operators is shown under this section.

Holiday Coach Tours 20 (J47636) is a Bedford with Duple bodywork in the white, red and blue livery of the company – the livery that was adopted when the three companies merged in 1993. The coach is seen parked at the old coach park opposite the Weighbridge bus station.

Tantivy Motors Tours was the last of the three companies, and the one whose name was taken to the forefront of the new company, which also used the Holiday Tours name again. Tantivy Motors 3 (J64338) is captured at the old coach park.

Mascot Motors 21 (J57347) is a Leyland Swift with Vanguard bodywork, one of three such coaches that were in the fleet at the time of the merger. The blue and cream livery would soon be gone from the island. The Seymour Group sold to concentrate on the hotel side of the business. The coach is seen in the old coach park.

# Pioneer Coaches

This coach operator, like the others, used Bedfords and Volkswagens for its coach fleet. They operated in a white livery with black fleet names. Pioneer Coaches had a contract with Condor Ferries in addition to providing the usual tours around the island and airport transfers. This operator was different from the others in that selected Saturday tours were operated in the afternoon. In 1993, the company purchased a double-deck bus and converted it to open-top to provide two daily tours. In doing this they brought back double-deck operation to the island, which last ran in the 1970s. Pioneer purchased a number of buses as it wanted to operate bus services in competition with JMT, but was refused a licence for this. The company also purchased an ex-London Transport RT with the intention of operating it, but this was found to need too much work to get it running again and was therefore sold to become a mobile home instead – the owner sold out to Tantivy Blue Coach Tours in 1999.

15 (J14610), ex-E962NMK, is one of a number of vehicles purchased from the UK to update its fleet of ageing Bedford coaches. This bus was modified before entering service, along with its sisters at Gatwick Engineering. It is seen carrying the new livery of black and white while on layover on its full-day tour at Greve de Lecq.

Pioneer was the first of the Jersey Companies to take the Cannon Islander into stock, this being one of three purchased new by the company. When the company sold out in 1999, it introduced the type to Tantivy Blue Coaches, who became the third operator of the class. 4 (J14616) is seen at Greve de Lecq.

16 (J14656, ex-E963NMK), sister vehicle to 15, seen earlier, is seen carrying the old white fleet livery with black fleet names. The coach is seen at the old coach park awaiting its use for the day.

18 (J14638) is a Leyland and was the first coach on the island to have a wheelchair lift; it had this livery applied to promote the fact. It is seen outside the JMT information office.

19 (J14640, ex-E742JAY), a mini-coach, is seen on a Saturday afternoon awaiting the arrival of holidaymakers to take them to the hotels on the island.

E182UWF is seen outside the depot as acquired. The company wanted to operate a network of bus services in competition with JMT, but was refused a licence for this by the authorities, which would later result in the company selling to JMT.

28 (J14097, ex-J176MCW), a Metrorider acquired from Ribble bus services, was another such vehicle purchased with the intentions of running bus services. It is seen heading back to the depot.

Pioneer started an open-top sightseeing tour in 1993 after it acquired this Leyland PD and converted it to open-top. Oliver (J14672) is seen shortly after departing from Liberation Square with a full load of happy tourists for one of two daily departures.

LUC394, ex-London Transport RT4045, was purchased with the intention of using it in service, but after some thought it was deemed uneconomical to repair and was instead sold to be used as a mobile home.

E (J39005) is a Volkswagen Transporter and is mainly used to ferry guests between hotels that have narrow roads and the full-sized coaches used for the main tours. It is seen outside the depot.

# Tantivy Holiday Tours and Tantivy Blue Coach Tours

Following the merger of the three companies in 1993, Tantivy Holiday Tours was now the biggest operator on the island. They operated in the white, red and blue former Holiday Tours livery. However, over the following years the fleet started to reduce in size due to the decline in tourists. This changed following the building of a couple of waterfront hotels and apartments, allowing an increase in tourist numbers. When Blue Coach Tours and Tantivy Holiday Tours merged, the company had around fifty coaches and minibuses. Then, in 1999, with the purchase of Pioneer Coaches, more modern coaches were used to update their own fleet, allowing ageing coaches to be withdrawn and disposed of along with some of the unsuitable ex-Pioneer vehicles. In September 2002, the company took on some of the former JMT school routes, using some of the buses. And in 2003 a new service was launched under the Easylink name, but this also took away some of the coach business from the company as the drivers were needed for this service since most of the bus drivers had transferred to Connex.

12 (J33630). A new livery was introduced by 1997 but only a handful of coaches received it, as Blue Coach Tours was then acquired and it was decided to use the later colour scheme for its livery. The coach is seen in the coach park near the Weighbridge bus station in St Helier.

20 (J75668) is seen at the airport having just dropped departing tourists off at the airport, and is driving round to the pick-up point to await the arrival of more visitors starting their holiday in the week leading up to the Battle of Flowers.

76 (J58927) is one of many old Bedford coaches that lasted in the fleet into the early 2000s. It is seen parked next to a similar Blue Coach Tours motor in the main coach car park in St Helier.

100 (J63875), a Leyland DAF mini-coach, was one of several owned by Tantivy when the companies merged in 1993, along with Volkswagen Transporters.

J7247 (JAB661) is a Bedford OB painted in the old Tantivy livery acquired to operate on a number of special tours advertised as 'Vintage Tours'. The coach was also used for wedding hires and took part in the annual Battle of Flowers parade.

1 (J82047) is a Camo-bodied Renault and is seen in St Helier taking passengers for a tour of the island.

3 (J39815) was the only Iveco coach within the fleet. It has a Swift body and is seen between trips carrying visitors leaving and arriving at the airport.

6 (41130) is a Leyland Elme. Having just dropped passengers at the airport, it's making its way to pick up arriving passengers and take them onwards to their hotels and guesthouses. This coach later went on to provide its chassis for a Battle of Flowers float.

15 (J24457) is a Leyland with a Vanguard body. It is leaving the airport with newly arrived visitors, who are welcomed by nice, sunny weather.

29 (J6380) is seen in the old Holiday Tours George Town depot prior to its closure and redevelopment as a housing estate. The site was used for engineering and the parking of withdrawn coaches in its last years as a depot. This coach was originally registered D832CNV with Gatwick Parking, Horley, and was one of two Caetano Aveiro Bedfords formerly with Holiday Tours as their 16.

49 (J64339) is seen passing the old Blue Coach's bus station, and is seen in this rather nice livery, which was only applied to a handful of coaches before the merger between the two companies. This and 33, seen in the background, have yet to gain their new fleet name.

59 (J84872) is one of the ex-Pioneer coaches that was acquired with the takeover of the company. It was used to replace ageing Bedfords within the fleet, which were the only Cannon's in the Tantivy Blue Coach fleet. It is seen departing Greve de Leqc with a full load and friendly driver.

62 (J32069) is seen here. Not all coaches would leave the airport with a full load, as some people would choose to stay at remote hotels away from St Helier for a more relaxing holiday.

64 (J90393) The airport was the best place to catch most of the coach fleets, especially on a Saturday or Wednesday as these were the two main change over days on the island. You needed to book your hotel guesthouse prior to booking your flights and transfers as there was a limited number of beds on the island. Tours did not run on a Saturday as all available drivers were needed to provide airport/ferry transfers.

65 (J73973) is seen along with sister vehicle 27(J87196), parked up before the driver returns to drive the coach round to the arrival point and pick up more visitors.

People are starting to queue at the rear of 68 (J14610) after being instructed by the driver which coach will be taking them on to their hotel. The driver will then return and put on the cases in order of drop off, making his life a lot easier when dropping off passengers as at some of the locations the drivers need to pull up on the street. This method minimises delays to traffic.

70 (J91574) is seen either returning from a school run or it is on a road test and returning to the harbour coach park.

131 (J14660), a Renault master midi-coach, awaits passengers at the airport on this Saturday in August 2003. Most of the visitors arriving will be heading to the Battle of Flowers on the coming Thursday.

# Waverley Coaches

This small coach operator also runs a programme of half- and full-day tours and excursions to the zoo and war tunnels. The owners of the company also owned the Norfolk Hotel and run additional excursions from there. The company moved from Gloucester Street to a location in Patriotic Street before moving to the former Pioneer Coach's premises at La Collette in the early 2000s, as the area around the old depots was redeveloped for offices.

2 (J51772) is one of four Leyland Swifts bought new by the company in March 1989. The company acquired a fifth in April 1996. These replaced the Bedfords with Duple bodywork from front-line duties. It is seen leaving the airport with another load of tourists on the way to their hotel or guesthouse.

7 (J79519) is a Renault Master midi-coach and is seen waiting to collect passengers from the airport on this warm Saturday afternoon.

9 (J57106), a Volkswagen Transporter, is seen transferring passengers and luggage to a Swift 3 for the start of their journey home.

12 (J37684), a Bedford Duple, is seen awaiting its driver and passengers for its tour of the island or attractions. It is seen at the coach park in St Helier.

A pair of Mercedes midi-coaches were purchased new and were the only two of their kind. 17 (J69526) is seen at the harbour awaiting passengers.

20 (J93812) is a Cannon Islander that was new in May 2001. Waverley was the second company to purchase a fleet of these coaches. This particular coach is seen at Greve de Lecq resting while its driver and passengers enjoy refreshments in the restaurant before continuing their tour.

22 (J87461), new in April 2002, is the newest coach in the fleet. It is seen approaching Greve de Lecq on one of the company tours on a nice sunny day.

# Other Transport Operators
# of Interest

## Les Petits Trains

Les Petits Trains operate a fleet of three trains across two routes. One train was used on a town tour, while the others operate between St Aubin's and Havre des Pas. Services operated hourly.

Lillie (J37990) is seen on the path by the beach wall, having made its way from St Aubin Bay. It is about to arrive at its terminal at the West Pier ready for its next departure.

## Puddle Duck Tours

Puddle Duck Tours provide a service linking West Pier and Elizabeth Castle, just off the coast of Havre des Pas.

Victory (J42159) shows the Second World War DUKWs as they were first used when I first visited the island. The company operated three such vehicles, and they later underwent a refurbishment programme. The image was taken at the West Pier, with the vehicle awaiting a departure to Elizabeth Castle.

## Special Tours

Special Tours operate a selection of three tours around the island for passengers from Germany, Switzerland and Austria, using three Ford Transit minibuses.

Special Tours used three of these Ford Transits on its network of tours from Sunday to Friday. They provided hotel transfers on a Saturday. This bus is pictured at the airport awaiting arrival of visitors to the island.

## Connex Jersey

A pale blue livery and blinds made the bus look a shade of white-blue. The most notable bus in the opening fleet was 247, an ex-Armchair Passenger Transport Dart that had arrived in its previous operator's livery from Dawson Rentals and placed into service. At the commencement of their bus services contract, twenty-three routes were operated. A new route – numbered 11 – was added for the summer 2003 timetable linking St Helier with the new waterfront and harbour. A total of thirty-three brand new Slimbus Dennis Darts were ordered, which had eleven fewer seats than the buses previously operated. It soon become clear that other buses needed to be sourced. The fleet numbering system was a little different in that the first number was the year the bus came into stock, with the new buses gaining fleet numbers 201–33. Some hired buses carried 2XX numbers until they were returned off lease. 247 was acquired and kept its fleet number. The buses acquired for the 2003 season took the number 334+, which included several ex-Armchair Passenger Transport Dennis Darts plus a number of hired Mercedes Benz Varios from Dawson Rentals.

The state of Jersey had a purpose-built depot that Connex operated the island's bus services from. It became operational from September 2002 with the start of the winter timetable.

201 (J101701) was the first of thirty-three Canteno Slimbus' delivered brand new for the company's network of services. It is seen operating town route 20 outside Weighbridge bus station. Note the number 2 at the front of the fleet number – the year the bus was new.

202 (J101702) is seen at Weighbridge bus station loading up passengers on route 2C.

205 (J101705) is seen loading passengers for route 7B on the first summer of the bus network under Connex.

207 (J101707) is seen departing Weighbridge on the new route 11, which linked the bus station with the harbour and the new waterfront leisure complex on a circular service. I took a journey on the route and was the only passenger on board.

210 (J101710) is seen at the airport having just dropped off its passengers. It waits 5 minutes before its return to St Helier while working on route 15.

211 (J101711) is seen with just a couple of passengers on board for its journey to the Devil's Hole tourist attraction on route 7.

212 (J101152) is seen loading up a healthy load of passengers on its journey via St Martin's Church on its way to Rozel Bay on route 3.

216 (J101216) is seen at the Living Legend tourist attraction while working route 8, awaiting departure back to St Helier.

Having worked its way from St Helier on route 1, 221 (J101721) is seen about to arrive at Gorey Pier.

222 (J101722) is allocated to town service 18, which uses two buses and connects the local estates to the town centre for shoppers and commuters alike. It also provides a handy link to the shops at the far side of town.

We see 225 (J101725) working route 21 – another local town service

227 (J101727) is seen about to depart Weighbridge bus station on route 12A.

229 (J101729) is seen on its way to St Brelade's Bay, calling at St Aubin to pick up more passengers. This stop is served by a several routes and the Ditto train.

231 (J101731) is seen at Greve de Lecq about to bring passengers back towards St Helier.

247 (J101747, ex-P159MLE) was the only Dart that was acquired from Dawson Rentals in 2002 – indicated by its fleet number starting with a 2. It was pressed into service in the former owner's livery – the Armchair Passenger Transport of Brentford, London. The bus is seen on route 14 at St Aubin while working to St Brelade's Bay.

Like 247, 334 (J101734, ex-P156MLE) was also acquired from Dawson Rentals and is a former Armchair vehicle. Note the number 3 indicates the bus joined the fleet in 2003.

339 (101739, ex-R989VU) was one of a ten Mercedes Varios hired to cover extra capacity for the 2003 summer season. It is seen about to perform a journey on route 1 to Gorey Pier with a fair load.

344 (J101744, ex-S390HVV) was another such vehicle hired. It is also awaiting departure to Gorey, but this time on route 1A.

346 (J100076, ex-T471HNH) was the final one of the hired batch of buses. It has Alexander bodywork and is seen with a fair load on its way to St Brelade's Bay on route 14.

## Easylink

A new hop-on/hop-off network of coach services operated by Tantivy Blue Coach Tours under the Easylink name used a fleet of twenty-six Dennis Darts from the former JMT fleet. The fleet numbers were 201–227 (again, not using the number 13, meaning there was no number 213 in the fleet). Providing a coach service to Jersey's attractions and bays across a network of four services, the company also operated former JMT school contracts. The livery was smart green and yellow colours, although not all buses were repainted at the start of the new operation and some operated in the former blue and white livery, while others had the blue painted green.

The four services that operated Sunday to Friday between 9.30 a.m. and 5.30 p.m. were as follows:

- Link 55: Weighbridge – Glass Church – Jersey War Tunnels – Living Legend – Grave de Lecq – Tresures of the Earth – Jersey Pearl – Watersplash – Corbiere – St Brelades Bay – St Aubin-Weighbridge. Every 30 mins.
- Link 66: Operates in the opposite direction to Link 55. Every 30 mins.
- Link 77: Weighbridge – Jersey Pottery – Gorey Pier – La Houge Bie – Jersey Zoo and return. Every 30 mins.
- Link 88: Weighbridge – Glass Church – Jersey War Tunnels – Living Legend – Jersey Gold – Jersey Zoo. Hourly.

The routes and fares of the services provided by Easylink are shown on these blackboards in the former Jersey Motor Transport offices and bus station.

201 (J93500, ex-CMN72X), a former Isle of Man vehicle and the former JMT 9, is still wearing the former JMT livery with the new Easylink fleet names. It is seen at the Living Legend on route 55 on its way to Greve de Lecq.

202 (J16861, ex-CMN77X) is another of the six former Isle of Man Darts that were bought by parent company JMT to replace older buses in the fleet. This was former JMT53 and had been repainted but had yet to receive the new fleet names in August 2003. It is seen at the Living Legend on route 66.

206 (J90454, ex-CMN79X), former JMT55, is seen approaching the Gorey Pier stop on its return from the zoo while working route 77.

206 (J90454) is seen at the Living Legend tourist attraction on its way to Jersey Zoo on route 88, and shows off the new bright livery introduced by Tantivy Blue coach tours for its hop-on/hop-off coach service.

208 (J46794), former JMT10, is seen returning from being parked up between trips on the Easylink service and is about to enter the bus station.

209 (J46631), former JMT8, is seen at the Living Legend with a full load while working route 55 on its way to Greve de Lecq on another hot August day in 2003.

Because Easylink services were a coach operation rather than a bus operation; the service had to pick up and drop off at the restaurant and not the bus stop at the top of the car coach park. 209 (J46631) is seen at Greve de Lecq.

211 (J46598), former JMT4, picks up and drops off at the coach park in Gorey while working route 77 on its way to the zoo.

212 (J75609), former JMT7, is seen having just dropped off its passengers. The driver is off for a break before he works another Easylink service.

217 (J84709), former JMT44, is seen departing Grave de Lecq while on its return journey to St Helier on route 66.

218 (J13853), former JMT11, is seen at the St Brelade's Parish Hall at St Aubin Bay as the coach services are unable to use the bus stop just behind the bus.

The driver of 219 (J74393), former JMT22, has his blind set for his next journey on the Easylink coach service while he goes to have a break on this hot summer's day.

221 (J86370), former JMT65, is seen heading to Weighbridge for the start of its journey on route 66 to Greve de Lecq. This was one of the buses to receive green over the old JMT blue, along with Easylink fleet names, until it could be repainted.

223 (J61334), former JMT40, is seen leaving Greve de Lecq with a handful of passengers on its way around the bay and attractions while returning to St Helier.

As mentioned previously, JMT provided duplicates if the services were full. This continued under the Easylink name, but because it was no longer part of the bus network, instead a hop-on coach service, the buses would show relief. This can be seen here on 223 (J61334), which is about to run an extra on service 55 from the coach station. These were needed due to the fact Connex had fewer seats on their buses and only a handful of spare buses to deal with the demand, plus you did not need to return to St Helier to continue to other locations on board Easylink services.

226 (J85325), former JMT68. I'm not sure why this bus was only going as far as St Ouen's Bay, but it can be seen departing the coach station at about 3.30 p.m. on this August afternoon.

227 (J11467), former JMT69, is the highest of the fleet. It is seen operating route 88 while stopping off at the Living Legend tourist attraction as it makes its way to St Helier.